A Crabtree Branches Book

EXTREME SPORTS

Skateboarding

Bernard Conaghan

Crabtree Publishing
crabtreebooks.com

School-to-Home Support for Caregivers and Teachers

This high-interest book is designed to motivate striving students with engaging topics while building fluency, vocabulary, and an interest in reading. Here are a few questions and activities to help the reader build upon his or her comprehension skills.

Before Reading:

- *What do I think this book is about?*
- *What do I know about this topic?*
- *What do I want to learn about this topic?*
- *Why am I reading this book?*

During Reading:

- *I wonder why...*
- *I'm curious to know...*
- *How is this like something I already know?*
- *What have I learned so far?*

After Reading:

- *What was the author trying to teach me?*
- *What are some details?*
- *How did the photographs and captions help me understand more?*
- *Read the book again and look for the vocabulary words.*
- *What questions do I still have?*

Extension Activities:

- *What was your favorite part of the book? Write a paragraph on it.*
- *Draw a picture of your favorite thing you learned from the book.*

Table of Contents

What Is Skateboarding?

Skateboarding is an **extreme** sport. Skateboarders ride through obstacles and perform tricks on **ramps**. Skateboarding first became popular in California in the 1950s, when surfers would use short surfboards with wheels attached to the bottom. The first **manufactured** skateboard was sold in stores in 1959.

Fun Fact

More than half of American skateboarders live in California.

Skateboarding in Action

Skateboarding is one of the most popular extreme sports in the world. There are many types of skateboarding styles. One style is **vertical**, or vert, skateboarding. This is where skateboarders do tricks on a nearly vertical ramp.

Цех

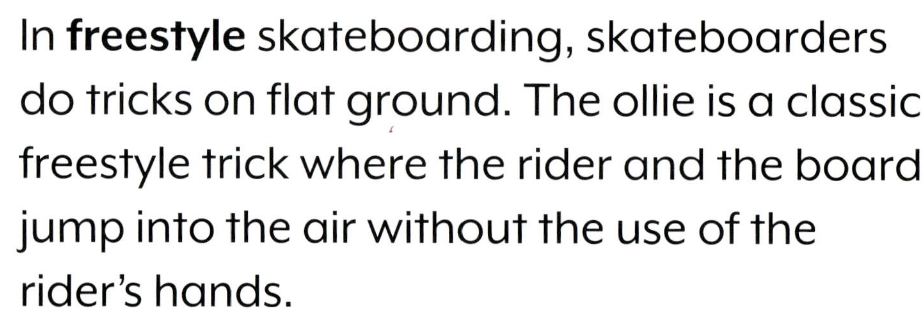

In **freestyle** skateboarding, skateboarders do tricks on flat ground. The ollie is a classic freestyle trick where the rider and the board jump into the air without the use of the rider's hands.

Fun Fact

Skateboarding used to be called sidewalk surfing.

In the 1950s, surfers would get out their skateboards when the waves were low and do the same tricks on the ground as they did surfing on the water.

Street skateboarding is done in an **urban** environment. Skateboarders use objects such as benches, stairs, or handrails to perform tricks. Kickflips and hardflips are two popular tricks in street skateboarding. However, street skateboarding is dangerous. Street skateboarders must be careful not to break things or **trespass**.

PRIVATE PROPERTY
NO TRESPASSING

Fun Fact

The first skate park was built in Arizona in 1965.

Park skateboarding is a combination of street and vert skateboarding. Skate parks have ramps, as well as obstacles such as stairs, ledges, and railings. This gives skateboarders a safe place to enjoy their sport.

Off-road skateboarding, or dirt boarding, is when skateboarders ride on rough ground. Gravel paths, BMX courses, woodlands, and mountain bike trails are common places to do off-road skateboarding.

Fun Fact

Longboards were invented in the 1950s.

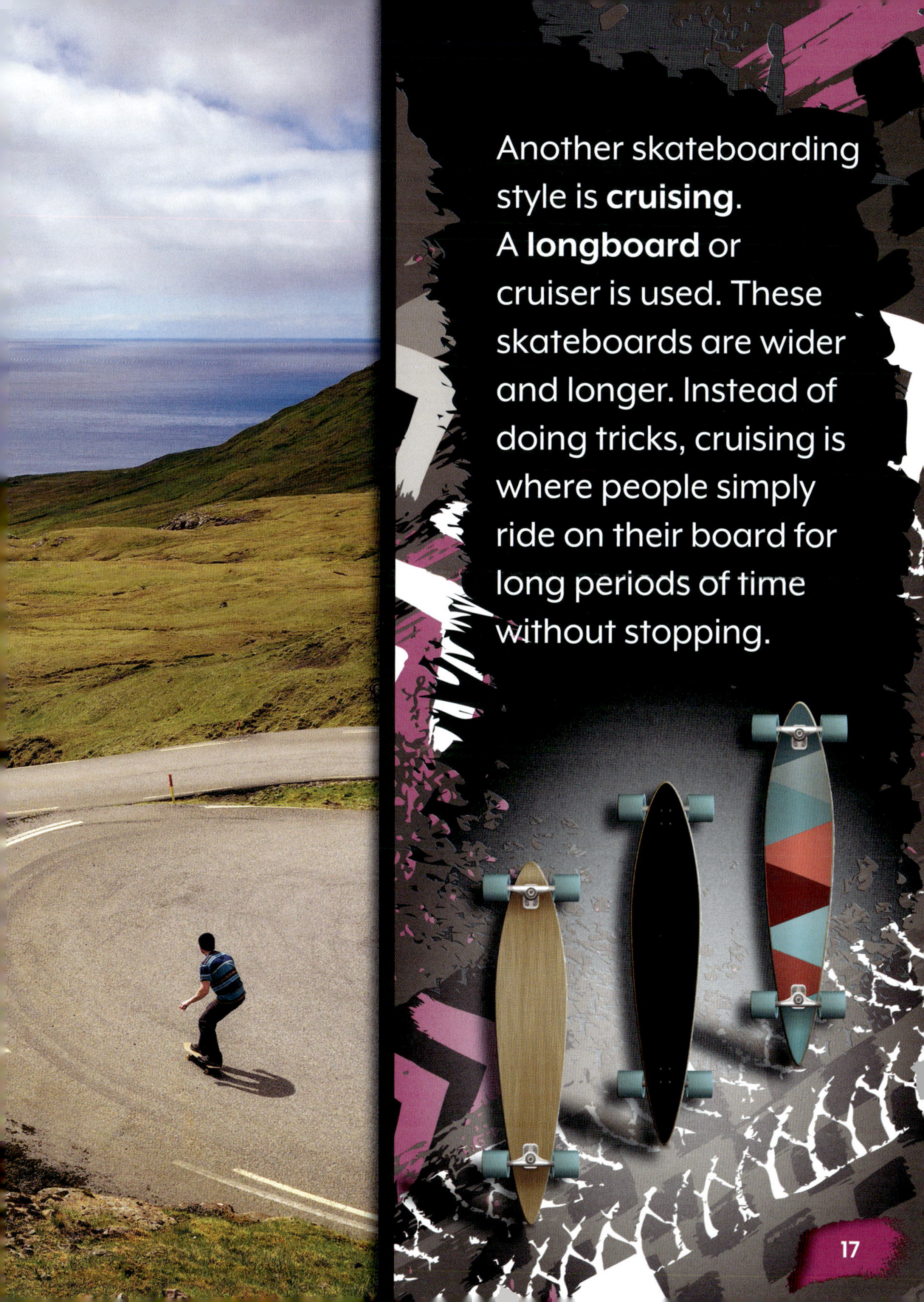

Another skateboarding style is **cruising**. A **longboard** or cruiser is used. These skateboards are wider and longer. Instead of doing tricks, cruising is where people simply ride on their board for long periods of time without stopping.

Parts of a Skateboard

The board part of a skateboard is called the **deck**. It is one of the most important parts of a skateboard as it is the part the skater stands on. Types of skateboards include longboards, cruisers, and shortboards.

Fun Fact

Decks are usually made of seven to nine layers of birch or maple wood.

The grip tape is the rough material on top of the skateboard deck. It is important because it helps the skateboarder's shoes to grip the board.

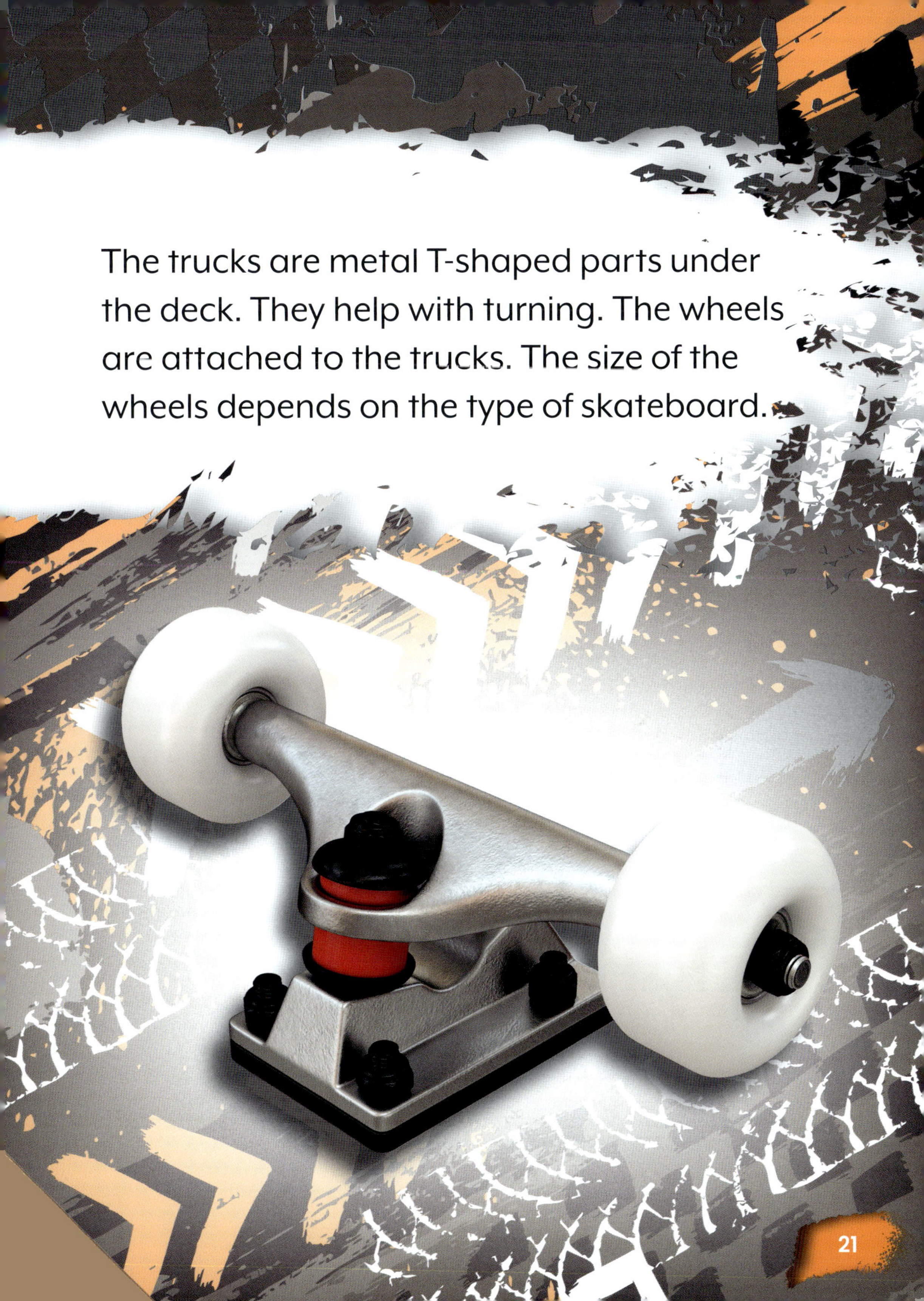

The trucks are metal T-shaped parts under the deck. They help with turning. The wheels are attached to the trucks. The size of the wheels depends on the type of skateboard.

Your Skateboarding Career

The best way to start competing in skateboarding is to go to your local skate park and start practicing. A coach can also help. Once you've learned the basic skills, a coach can teach you tricks and increase your skill level.

Fun Fact

Sports in the X Games include skateboarding, motocross, skiing, and snowboarding.

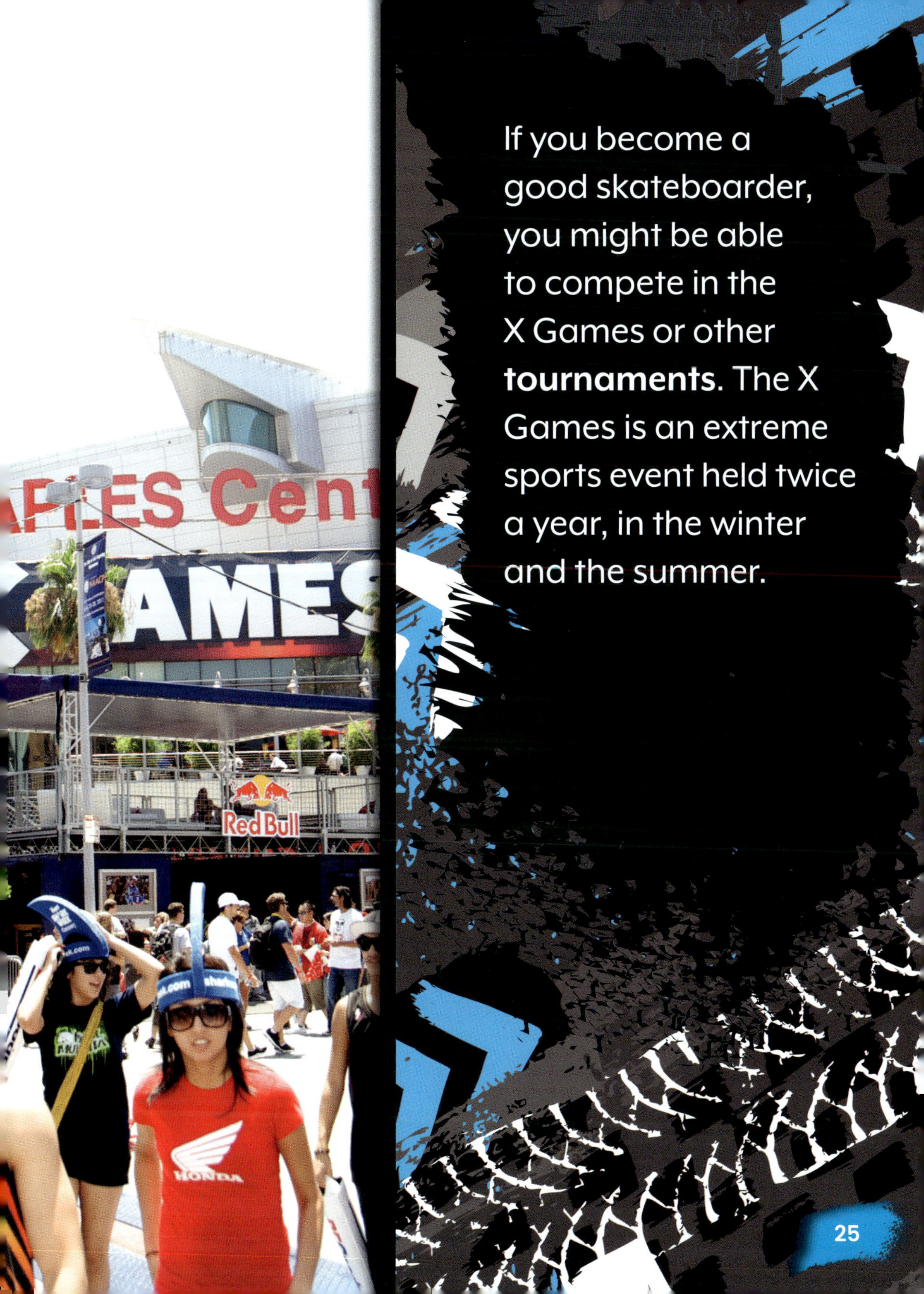

If you become a good skateboarder, you might be able to compete in the X Games or other **tournaments**. The X Games is an extreme sports event held twice a year, in the winter and the summer.

Skateboarding Legends

Throughout the history of skateboarding there have been many different **legends**. One of them is Tony Hawk. He is a 12-time National Skateboarding Association vert champion. He was born on May 12, 1968, in Carlsbad, California.

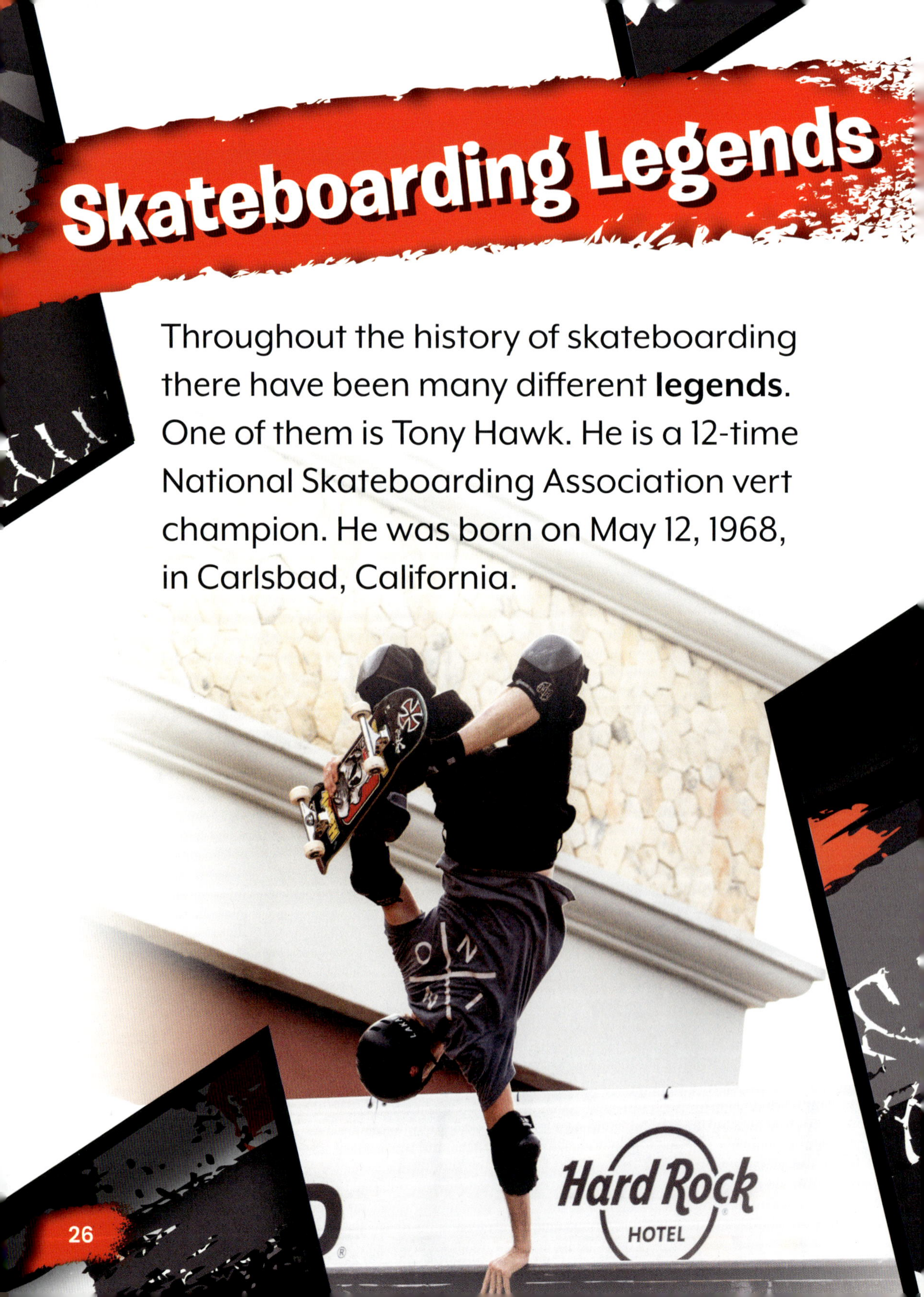

Fun Fact

Hawk started surfing before skateboarding, but is scared of big waves.

Another legend is Leticia Bufoni. She has won a total of 12 X Game medals. Six of them are gold. She is also the 2015 female skateboarding world champion. Bufoni is the first female to sign with Nike Skateboarding. She was born on April 13, 1993, in São Paulo, Brazil.

Fun Fact

Bufoni has won the most medals of any woman in the summer X Games.

Glossary

cruising (KROO·zihng): Moving at a steady speed for a long period of time

deck (DEK): The flat part of the skateboard where the rider stands

extreme (ek·STREEM): Something that is far beyond the normal

freestyle (FREE·stile): In sports, a performance or competition in which participants are allowed to use different styles or methods

legend (LEH·jind): Someone who is famous and admired for doing something well

longboard (LAWNG·bord): A longer version of a skateboard

manufactured (MAN-yoo-fak-churd): Something that is made in large amounts by using machines

ramp (RAMP): A piece of equipment with a slope

tournament (TUR·nuh·ment): A competition with many participants

trespass (TREH·spas): To enter somewhere without permission

urban (UR-buhn): Relating to a city

vertical (VUR-ti-kuhl): Going straight up and down

Index

Websites to Visit

www.xgames.com

www.redbull.com/us-en/hubs/skateboarding

https://olympics.com/en/sports/skateboarding/

About the Author

Bernard Conaghan lives in South Carolina with his German shepherd named Duke. Every year he goes snowboarding in Switzerland. He is a coach on his son's football team. He always eats one scoop of peach ice cream after dinner.

Written by: Bernard Conaghan
Designed by: Jen Bowers
Series Development: James Earley
Proofreader: Melissa Boyce
Educational Consultant: Marie Lemke M.Ed.

Photographs: Cover image ©2021 Andrey Burmakin/Shutterstock, background ©Matisson_ART/Shutterstock; p.3 ©2009 taboga/Shutterstock; p.4 ©2021 Andrey Burmakin/Shutterstock; p.5 © Parrot Ivan/Shutterstock;p.6 ©2017 SAPhotog/Shutterstock; p.7 ©2017 hurricanehank/Shutterstock, phone ©2017 Vasin Lee/Shutterstock; p.8 ©2017 mimagephotography/Shutterstock; p.9 ©2021 TnkImages/Shutterstock; p.11 ©2013 Frenzel/Shutterstock; p.12 ©2021 tytokyo/Shutterstock; p.13 ©2021 paulzhuk/Shutterstock; p.15 ©2020 wbilek/Shutterstock; p.16 ©2019 Nick Fox/Shutterstock; p.17 ©Adazhiy Dmytro/Shutterstock; p.18 ©2015 Dudarev Mikhail/Shutterstock, ©2022 Salamahin/Shutterstock; p.19 ©2015 Tamisclao/Shutterstock; p.21 ©2022 Salamahin/Shutterstock; p.22 ©2018 oneinchpunch/Shutterstock; p.23 ©2014 mooinblack/Shutterstock; p.24 ©2011 Juan Camilo Bernal/Shutterstock; p.25 medals ©Net Vector/Shutterstock; p.26 ©2019 Arturo Verea/Shutterstock; p.27 ©2011 EpicStockMedia/Shutterstock; p.29 ©2021 A.RICARDO/Shutterstock

Crabtree Publishing

crabtreebooks.com 800-387-7650

Printed in the U.S.A./012023/CG20220815

Published in Canada
Crabtree Publishing
616 Welland Avenue
St. Catharines, Ontario
L2M 5V6

Published in the United States
Crabtree Publishing
347 Fifth Avenue
Suite 1402-145
New York, New York 10016

Library and Archives Canada Cataloguing in Publication
Available at Library and Archives Canada

Library of Congress Cataloging-in-Publication Data
Available at the Library of Congress

Hardcover: 978-1-0396-9664-8
Paperback: 978-1-0396-9771-3
Ebook (pdf): 978-1-0396-9985-4
Epub: 978-1-0396-9878-9